FRILLED LIZARD

HARLEQUIN POISON
DART FROG

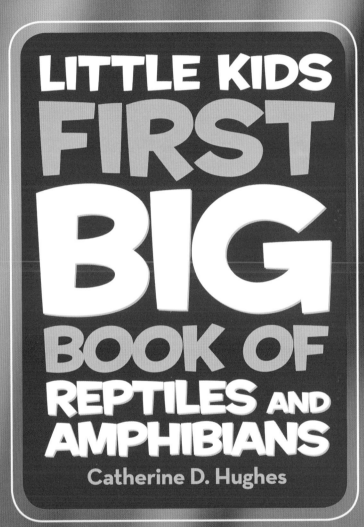

# LITTLE KIDS
# FIRST
# BIG
# BOOK OF
# REPTILES AND
# AMPHIBIANS

Catherine D. Hughes

NATIONAL
GEOGRAPHIC
KiDS

WASHINGTON, D.C.

# CONTENTS

KOMODO DRAGON

PANTHER CHAMELEON

# CHAPTER FOUR

# CHAPTER FIVE

EYELASH
VIPER

DYEING POISON
DART FROG

# INTRODUCTION

This book introduces readers to the world of reptiles and amphibians. It answers questions that range from "What is an amphibian?" and "What is the biggest reptile in the world?" to "How can a boa constrictor fit a deer into its mouth?" The first chapter introduces the topic of reptiles and amphibians. The next three chapters feature groups of reptiles, and the last chapter highlights a selection of amphibians.

**CHAPTER ONE** begins the book with a look at what makes an animal a reptile or an amphibian. Photographs and text combine to describe reptiles' general physical and behavioral characteristics. Amphibians are presented next, and compared to and contrasted with reptiles.

**CHAPTER TWO** introduces snakes, lizards, and the one-of-a-kind reptile the tuatara. Readers will enjoy an overview of this group of reptiles, from garter snakes to Komodo dragons. Colorful photo galleries reinforce the wide range of species.

**CHAPTER THREE** explores the world of turtles and tortoises. Descriptions of the way each animal is adapted to its environment give the reader a peek into the topic of wildlife diversity.

**CHAPTER FOUR** examines an ancient group of reptiles: crocodilians. Here readers will experience a cross section of species representing the main types of crocodilians: alligators and caimans, crocodiles, and gharials.

**CHAPTER FIVE** takes a look at amphibians and features frogs, toads, salamanders, and the unusual caecilian. More photo galleries help illustrate the diversity of amphibians.

# HOW TO USE THIS BOOK

**FACT BOXES** for each featured species give readers a quick overview, including range, diet, number of young, and size. An animal's size is compared with a five-year-old child's height, hand, or foot (depending on the size of the animal).

**COLORFUL PHOTOGRAPHS** illustrate each spread and support the text. Galleries showcase the diversity of species for both reptiles and amphibians.

**POP UP FACTS** sprinkled throughout provide added information about the reptiles and amphibians featured in each section.

**INTERACTIVE QUESTIONS** in each section encourage conversation related to the topic.

In the back of the book, **MORE FOR PARENTS** offers fun activities that relate to reptiles and amphibians, as well as a helpful **GLOSSARY.**

# CHAPTER 1
# FEATURED CREATURES

YACARÉ
CAIMANS

More than 10,000 different species, or kinds, of reptiles live around the world. About 8,000 species of amphibians share the planet. In this chapter, discover what makes an animal a reptile or an amphibian.

# WHAT ARE REPTILES?

EMERALD TREE BOA

Reptiles are a group of animals that includes snakes, lizards, turtles, alligators, and crocodiles. Reptiles are vertebrates. This means they are animals that have a spine, or backbone. You are a vertebrate, too! But you are not a reptile. You are a mammal.

Reptiles are also ectotherms. An ectotherm is an animal that cannot produce its own heat. Its body temperature changes with the temperature around it. Reptiles warm themselves in sunlight. They move into shade to cool off.

**EASTERN BOX TURTLE**

**PLUMED BASILISK**

Mammals, including humans, are **ENDOTHERMS.** An endotherm's body can **PRODUCE** its own **HEAT,** no matter what the **TEMPERATURE** is around it.

11

Most reptiles are covered with scales,
shells, or bony plates. They usually
have claws on their toes.

It takes about
**THREE** months
for marine iguana
**EGGS** to **HATCH.**
Buried in the
**SAND,** the eggs
stay warm.

A few reptiles give birth to live young, but most lay eggs.

Either way, newly born or hatched reptiles look like miniature versions of their parents. Baby reptiles can move around right away. They can find their own food and mostly take care of themselves without their parents' help.

GREEN SEA TURTLE HATCHING

NILE CROCODILE BABY AND MOTHER

13

As a group, reptiles live in a lot of different habitats. These include deserts, grasslands, forests, woodlands, meadows, and wetlands around the world. Reptiles do not live in places where it is always cold, like Antarctica.

Most reptiles live on land, but there are some—like sea turtles—that spend most of their lives in water.

**KEMP'S RIDLEY SEA TURTLE**

**GOLD DUST
DAY GECKO**

**EASTERN
GARTER
SNAKE**

**DWARF
CROCODILE**

COMMON FROG

# WHAT ARE AMPHIBIANS?

Amphibians are a group of animals that includes frogs, salamanders, and caecilians (sih-SIL-yens). Like reptiles, amphibians are air-breathing vertebrates and ectotherms.

FIRE
SALAMANDER

Most salamanders and caecilians are **QUIET**, but almost all frogs use **LOUD CALLS** to find mates and defend their territory.

Unlike reptiles, amphibians have smooth or warty skin, and they do not have claws.

Most amphibians breathe air like humans do, but they also breathe through their skin. Their skin needs to stay moist, so they live near water. Most amphibians live at least part of their lives in the water. Others live in water all the time.

STRIPED
CAECILIAN

17

A mother frog lays her eggs in or near water.

**1**

EGGS

**2**

When the eggs hatch, out pop tadpoles! They live underwater.

Amphibians lay eggs. Many lay their eggs in water. These amphibians hatch as larvae—babies that do not yet look like their parents and that develop underwater. For example, a frog starts out as a tadpole, which usually lives in water.

As a tadpole gets bigger, it grows legs. Its tail gets smaller and smaller.

3

4

When amphibian **LARVAE** grow large enough, they change into **ADULTS.** This change is called **METAMORPHOSIS.**

Finally, the tadpole looks like a frog. Most frogs leave the water.

A few kinds of amphibians lay their eggs in moist areas on land. These amphibians have larvae that stay inside their eggs until they change into adults.

19

Amphibians usually live where there is water, such as a pond or a stream, nearby. Some live in moist places like the wet leaves that cover the ground in many rainforests. Like reptiles, amphibians do not live in Antarctica, where it is always frozen. A few amphibians live where it is dry, but they stay underground until it rains.

ALPINE SALAMANDER

GREEN SALAMANDER

AFRICAN CLAWED FROG

BULLFROG

COMMON
WATER FROG

JAPANESE FIRE-
BELLIED NEWT

# CHAPTER 2
# SLITHER AND SCOOT

**PANTHER CHAMELEON**

This chapter begins with snakes, moves on to lizards, and ends with a one-of-a-kind reptile.

# COMMON
# GARTER SNAKE

## Garter snakes come in many colors.

## FACTS

**HOME**
most habitats, usually near water, in much of the U.S. and Canada, and in parts of Mexico

**FOOD**
earthworms, fish, amphibians, and other small animals

**BABIES**
7 to 20 at a time, born live

**SIZE**

**MALE GARTER** snakes are usually **SMALLER** than **FEMALES.**

A common garter snake can give birth to up to **80 BABY SNAKES** at one time, but it usually has no more than **20.**

Garter snakes live in grasslands and forests, lawns and fields. They eat many kinds of small animals.

Because they are so good at living in a lot of different places and eating a lot of different things, you might spot a garter snake almost anywhere in North America.

Most snakes hatch from eggs. But garter snake babies are born live. They leave their mother's body as little snakes, ready to slither!

**If you were a snake, what colors would you like to be?**

# ARIZONA CORAL SNAKE

## This snake is pretty but dangerous.

The Arizona coral snake's bright bands of color warn enemies that it is dangerous and to stay away. All snakes have teeth and can bite. Some snakes, like the Arizona coral snake, are venomous.

A venomous snake has two special teeth called fangs. When it bites an animal, the snake injects a powerful liquid called venom through its sharp fangs and into its prey.

The venom either kills the prey or makes it unable to move. Then the snake can swallow it whole.

Animals that **HUNT** are called **PREDATORS.** The animals they eat are called **PREY.**

## WHICH IS WHICH?

A few other kinds of snakes—including some kinds of king snakes and milk snakes—have bright bands of color similar to the coral snake's. But king and milk snakes are not venomous. Their colors protect them from getting eaten by predators that mistake these harmless snakes for the dangerous coral snake.

**ARIZONA CORAL SNAKE**

**SCARLET KING SNAKE**

**WESTERN MILK SNAKE**

The longest cobra known could **STRETCH HALFWAY UP** a telephone pole.

When a king cobra feels threatened, it **RAISES ITS HEAD** and the front part of its body straight up into the air.

**FACTS**

**HOME**
forests in India and Southeast Asia

**FOOD**
mostly other snakes

**BABIES**
12 to 51 eggs at a time

**SIZE**

# KING COBRA

## This is the world's longest venomous snake.

King cobras hunt for prey during the day. They attack prey with a bite, and their venom, delivered through their fangs, kills it.

The female king cobra builds a nest for her eggs. She guards them until they hatch. Then the young are on their own right away. The baby snakes are just as venomous as their parents.

The **KING COBRA** is one of the very few kinds of snakes that **MAKE NESTS.**

Why do you think a king cobra tries to look big when it feels threatened?

# BOA CONSTRICTOR

## A boa gives its prey a big squeeze.

The boa constrictor grabs its prey with its mouth, which is full of teeth. But this snake is not venomous. The boa kills by wrapping its body around and around its prey. It constricts, or squeezes, the animal until it is dead.

Then the boa fits the whole meal into its mouth. A snake can open its mouth very wide. Muscles move the meal down into the snake's stomach.

After eating a big meal, such as a small deer, a boa may not eat again for months.

A **NEWBORN BOA** would fit across this **OPEN BOOK**.

A **LARGE BOA** could easily stretch from the floor to the **CEILING** of most rooms.

## FACTS

**HOME**
forests and grasslands, from northern Mexico through much of South America

**FOOD**
small mammals, birds, reptiles, and amphibians

**BABIES**
10 to 64 at a time, born live

**SIZE**

# What is the biggest animal you have ever seen?

## FACTS

**HOME**
forests, woods, grass-lands, and wetlands in the southeastern U.S.

**FOOD**
rabbits, rats, birds, insects, and other small animals

**BABIES**
7 to 21 at a time, born live

**SIZE**

The eastern diamondback **RATTLESNAKE** is the largest **VENOMOUS** snake in the United States.

Can you name other things that make a rattling sound?

The diamondback gets its **NAME** from the **DIAMOND-SHAPED** pattern of **SCALES** on its back.

# EASTERN DIAMONDBACK
# RATTLESNAKE
## This snake shakes its noisy tail.

A rattlesnake's tail ends in segments, or bits, of keratin—the same material that your fingernails are made of. These hard bits of keratin form a rattle. The snake shakes its rattle to warn enemies to stay away. The noise sounds like a fast buzzing or rattling.

Like all snakes, a rattlesnake sheds its skin as it grows. New skin grows underneath the old. The old skin splits, and the snake wriggles out of it. The new skin fits its bigger body.

Each time a rattlesnake sheds its skin, a new segment of rattle is added to its tail.

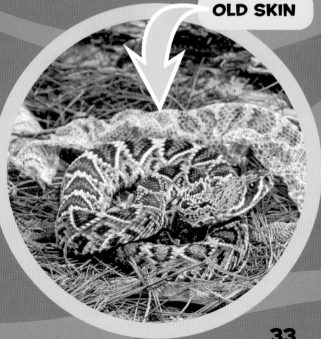

OLD SKIN

# BANDED SEA KRAIT

## Sea kraits hunt for food in the ocean.

This venomous snake spends about half its time in the ocean and the other half on land. It hunts, mostly for eels, in the ocean. Its tail is shaped like a paddle, which helps the sea krait swim. It moves its tail from side to side through the water.

A sea krait comes ashore to find a mate, lay eggs, shed its skin, and digest food.

**SAY MY NAME:** SEE KRATE

**FACTS**

**HOME**
coastal land, islands, and coral reefs in the western Pacific Ocean and eastern Indian Ocean

**FOOD**
mostly eels and some small fish

**BABIES**
4 to 20 eggs at a time

**SIZE**

SHARKS and SEA BIRDS prey on SEA KRAITS.

Can you think of three or more words that rhyme with krait? Hint: late ...

You've met some of the more than **3,000 SPECIES OF SNAKES.** Here are a few more.

BRAHMINY BLIND SNAKE

SRI LANKAN PIT VIPER

ASIAN VINE SNAKE

GREEN ANACONDA

GREEN TREE PYTHON

BRAZILIAN RAINBOW BOA

RED-HEADED KRAIT

# GREEN IGUANA
## This lizard uses its tail like a whip.

**FACTS**

**HOME**
rainforests of Central and South America; Caribbean islands

**FOOD**
leaves, flowers, and fruit

**BABIES**
10 to 30 eggs at a time

**SIZE**

A green iguana can have **SEVERAL COLORS** on its body, including **BLUE,** lavender, pink, black, and orange.

The green iguana is an arboreal lizard. This means it lives mostly in trees. It usually moves slowly, munching on leaves and flowers.

But if a predator—such as an eagle or a snake—approaches, a green iguana can move fast. If water is nearby, the iguana dives in and swims off.

The lizard can also defend itself by spreading out its dewlap, a flap of skin under its chin. It hisses while bobbing its head up and down. It can also whack an enemy with its spiny tail, swipe with sharp claws, or bite.

**What are some things you like to climb?**

# GREEN ANOLE
## This little lizard can change colors.

The green anole is usually green when it is calm, healthy, and warm. But when it is scared, sick, or cold, it is often dark brown.

The temperature and humidity, or the amount of water in the air, can also cause a green anole to change color.

**FACTS**

**HOME**
swamps, forests, and woods in the southeastern U.S.

**FOOD**
flies, crickets, moths, other small insects; worms and slugs

**BABIES**
15 to 18 eggs, laid one at a time every two weeks

**SIZE**

Like the green iguana, the green anole has a **DEWLAP.** The male's is usually **BRIGHT PINK.** The female's is **PALE PINK.**

**DEWLAP**

When a green anole hatches, it is only about as long as a **HUMAN BABY'S PINKIE FINGER.**

Anoles have special **PADS ON THEIR TOES** that help them scurry **STRAIGHT UP** trees, rocks, and walls.

If you could change color with your mood, what color would you be when you are happy?

# FRILLED LIZARD

## The frill on this lizard is its secret weapon.

OWLS, large **SNAKES**, and **FOXES** prey on frilled lizards.

**FRILLED** lizards are part of a group of **LIZARDS** called **DRAGONS.**

This lizard has a special trick for escaping predators. It opens its mouth—wide! That does two things.

First, the inside of the lizard's mouth, which is bright pink or yellow, surprises the predator. Second, the lizard's big neck frill pops open.

The mouth and frill trick, along with the frilled lizard's loud hissing, often startles the predator just long enough for the lizard to escape. Or the trick might scare the predator so much that it runs away!

**Frilled lizards often RUN on the GROUND from one tree to another on their HIND LEGS.**

**Can you name a time when something surprised you?**

## FACTS

**HOME**
grassy woodlands, dry forests in northern Australia, and southern New Guinea

**FOOD**
mostly insects; sometimes small mammals

**BABIES**
4 to 13 eggs at a time

**SIZE**

43

# PANTHER CHAMELEON

This lizard's eyes can move separately.

## FACTS

**HOME**
forests in parts of Madagascar, an island off the coast of Africa

**FOOD**
mostly insects

**BABIES**
10 to 46 eggs at a time

**SIZE**

A chameleon's **TONGUE** can be as long as its **BODY.**

A panther chameleon's eyes can look in two different directions at once. One eye might look up while the other eye looks to one side—each eye searching for prey.

But when this lizard spots an insect to eat, both eyes focus on it. *Zap!* Its tongue shoots out of its mouth and hits its target.

The end of the lizard's tongue is covered in a gooey glob of mucus. The prey sticks to it. The chameleon brings its tongue back into its mouth. The insect becomes a meal.

A panther chameleon's **TOES** help it **GRIP BRANCHES TIGHTLY.**

**What are some things you can pick up with your toes?**

# TOKAY GECKO

## A gecko can regrow its lost tail.

Swooping down from the sky, an owl grabs a tokay gecko by its tail—but the gecko gets away! Its tail comes off its body. The hawk is left hanging onto a wiggling tail while the lizard scurries away to safety. The gecko, like many kinds of lizards, can grow a new tail.

**NEW TAIL**

A tokay gecko's toes have **TINY HAIRS** that work like **SUCTION CUPS.** They help the lizard walk up walls and across ceilings.

Unlike most lizards, the tokay gecko makes very **LOUD CROAKING CALLS.**

## FACTS

**HOME**
cliffs, tropical forests, and near and in people's homes throughout Southeast Asia

**FOOD**
mostly cockroaches, locusts, and other insects; other small animals

**BABIES**
1 or 2 eggs at a time

**SIZE**

Many people who live where geckos are found happily share their homes with the lizards. The geckos eat pesky insects that people do not want around. The houses give the lizards shelter. It is a good partnership.

**Would you like to have a gecko living in your house? Why or why not?**

# GREAT
# DESERT SKINK

## These reptiles live in family groups.

A great desert **SKINK'S TAIL** is a little **LONGER** than its **BODY.**

**FACTS**

**HOME**
deserts in parts of Australia

**FOOD**
insects, spiders, and small lizards; some flowers, leaves, and fruit

**BABIES**
1 to 7 babies at a time, born live

**SIZE**

Skinks are lizards. There are many species, or kinds, of skinks. Great desert skinks are unusual because they live in family groups. Most skinks do not live in groups. Young great desert skinks live with their parents, brothers, and sisters until they are adults.

Great desert skinks dig big burrows in the sand to live in. A maze of tunnels connects several different rooms—including a bathroom! A burrow can be as long as a typical school bus. About 10 skinks live in a burrow at the same time.

A great desert **SKINK BURROW** can have as many as **20 ENTRANCES.**

**Can you name some other animals that live in Australia?**

# SAND LIZARD

## Male sand lizards change color.

Sand lizards are generally brown with black markings. But during a couple of months each year, in the spring, the male lizards become bright green. Female sand lizards that are ready for a mate notice the bright green males.

After the sun sets, the temperature cools down. The lizards stay still inside their burrows. When the sun rises, the temperature warms up the lizards. They start moving around to look for food.

FEMALE sand lizards lay their eggs in SUNNY, sandy spots. The sun keeps the EGGS WARM until they hatch.

During the cold winter, sand lizards hibernate in their burrows. They stay in a deep sleep until spring.

Sand lizard **BABIES** are **ON THEIR OWN** as soon as they **HATCH.**

**FACTS**

**HOME**
grasslands, meadows, and sand dunes in parts of Europe and Asia

**FOOD**
insects

**BABIES**
4 to 14 eggs at a time

**SIZE**

How many green animals can you name?

Until they are about four years old, **BABY** Komodo dragons spend much of their time in **TREES.**

## FACTS

**HOME**
forests and savannas on a few small islands in Indonesia

**FOOD**
wild pigs, water buffalo, deer, many smaller animals, and carrion (dead animals)

**BABIES**
25 eggs at a time

**SIZE**

# KOMODO DRAGON

## This creature is the largest lizard in the world.

The Komodo dragon got its name because it reminded people of a fire-breathing, storybook dragon. Like a make-believe dragon, this lizard is big. It also has a large yellow tongue. This tongue made people think of flames shooting out of a dragon's mouth.

Komodo dragons belong to a **GROUP** of animals called **MONITOR LIZARDS.**

This huge lizard has a big appetite and hunts large animals, like deer. A Komodo dragon can eat 180 pounds (82 kg) at one meal. That would be like you eating 720 hamburgers for dinner!

**Can you make up a story about a fire-breathing dragon?**

# MARINE IGUANA

## These lizards sneeze a lot!

A marine iguana can **HOLD ITS BREATH** underwater for **AN HOUR.**

Marine iguanas are lizards that find their food in the ocean. They use their teeth to scrape algae off rocks in the sea.

As they eat, the iguanas swallow a lot of salt from the ocean water. They need to get rid of this salt because too much in their bodies would make them sick.

As they rest and warm up on shore, the iguanas sneeze out the salt. *Achoo!* This salt turns the rocks around them white. It makes the lizards' heads white, too!

**FACTS**

**HOME**
rocky shoreline in the Galápagos Islands

**FOOD**
algae

**BABIES**
1 to 6 eggs at a time

**SIZE**

**SLITHER AND SCOOT**

Iguanas are the **ONLY LIZARDS** in the world that **FEED UNDERWATER** in the ocean.

Marine iguanas become **COLD QUICKLY** as they feed in the ocean. They must crawl back onto shore **TO WARM THEMSELVES** on **SUNNY** rocks.

**Would you rather swim in the ocean or in a pool? Why?**

There are more than **4,500 KINDS OF LIZARDS.** You have already met a few, including iguanas, anoles, chameleons, geckos, and skinks. Here are a few more lizard species.

EMERALD SWIFT

BLUE ANOLE

GILA MONSTER

SLOWWORM (A LEGLESS LIZARD)

RAINBOW AGAMA

# TUATARA

## This rare reptile can live to be 100 years old.

Tuataras have **EXISTED** since the time of the **DINOSAURS.**

**HOME**
open areas with few trees on islands off the coast of New Zealand

**FOOD**
spiders, beetles, frogs, small reptiles, and bird eggs

**BABIES**
5 to 18 eggs at a time

**SIZE**

The tuatara looks like a lizard, but it is not a lizard. Its teeth, ears, and other parts of its body are different. The tuatara is a one-of-a-kind reptile.

A female tuatara lays her eggs in a shallow hole that she digs in a sunny spot. She doesn't incubate, or keep them warm, herself. Instead, she covers the eggs with leaves and grass and walks away.

It takes the eggs more than a year to hatch. Like many reptiles, male and female tuataras develop depending on the temperature inside a nest. Nests in warmer spots produce males; cooler nests produce females.

Unlike other reptiles, a tuatara's **LOWER** row of **TEETH FITS** between the **UPPER TWO ROWS** when its mouth is closed.

**Who is the oldest person you know?**

59

# CHAPTER 3
# UNDER SHELLS

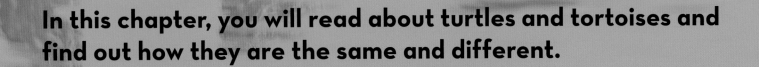

In this chapter, you will read about turtles and tortoises and
find out how they are the same and different.

# WHAT ARE TURTLES?

Turtles are reptiles with shells. Some turtles spend most of their time in water. They are aquatic turtles. Other turtles spend most of their time on land. They are terrestrial turtles and are often called tortoises.

Aquatic turtles tend to have flatter and lighter shells than those of terrestrial turtles. Aquatic turtles have webbed feet. The shape of their shells and their webbed feet make swimming easier.

Tortoises and other terrestrial turtles have rounded shells. Their feet have short claws and are not webbed.

Sea turtles rarely leave the **OCEAN.** Their feet are shaped like **PADDLES,** which they use to **SWIM.**

GREEN
SEA TURTLE

PADDLES

A turtle cannot **CRAWL** out of its shell. The **SHELL** is part of its **BODY.**

The top part of a **TURTLE'S SHELL** is called the **CARAPACE.** The bottom is called the **PLASTRON.**

**EASTERN SPINY SOFTSHELL TURTLE**

# HAWKSBILL
# SEA TURTLE

## Sea turtles nest on beaches.

**SIX OTHER SEA TURTLES** swim the world's **OCEANS:** the loggerhead, leatherback, Kemp's ridley, green, olive ridley, and flatback.

Hawksbill sea turtles can be found in ocean waters around the world. Like other sea turtles, male hawksbills never come ashore. Female sea turtles only come ashore to make nests and lay eggs.

First, the female hawksbill digs a hole in the sand with her back flippers. Then, she lays her eggs in the hole and covers them all with sand. She returns to the ocean and swims away.

Sixty days later, the eggs hatch. The baby turtles dig their way out of the nest. Then they scurry into the sea.

## FACTS

**HOME**
shallow coastal waters and reefs in tropical Pacific, Atlantic, and Indian Oceans

**FOOD**
mostly sea sponges

**BABIES**
100 to 140 eggs at a time

**SIZE**

The hawksbill sea turtle gets its name from the **SHAPE OF ITS BEAK,** which looks like a **HAWK'S BEAK.**

## Can you memorize and then name the seven species of sea turtles?

# ALLIGATOR SNAPPING TURTLE

## This turtle's tongue plays tricks on prey.

Alligator snapping turtles rarely **LEAVE** the **WATER.** Females come **ASHORE** only to **LAY EGGS.**

An alligator snapping turtle can stay underwater for up to 50 minutes before it must come to the surface to breathe. Its dark shell blends in with the mud at the bottom of a river. It lies there perfectly still, with its mouth open and its bright pink tongue wiggling.

Turtles do not have **TEETH.** Instead, they have **BEAKS** that they use to **CUT AND SLICE** their food.

**FACTS**

**HOME**
rivers, lakes, and swamps in the southeastern U.S.

**FOOD**
fish and other small animals; aquatic plants

**BABIES**
8 to 52 eggs at a time

**SIZE**

The wiggling tongue fools fish into thinking it is a tasty worm. As a fish moves in to grab the "worm," the alligator snapping turtle snaps its jaws shut. Now the fish is the turtle's dinner!

TONGUE

**Can you wiggle your tongue like a snapping turtle?**

# PAINTED TURTLE

This turtle's shell looks like it was decorated with yellow and red paint.

When they are cold, painted turtles crawl out of the water and onto a log or rock to sun themselves.

Painted turtles have many predators. Adult turtles must watch out for alligators, raccoons, and birds of prey, such as hawks, owls, and eagles. Little baby turtles, which are on their own from the time they hatch, can also be gobbled up by fish, frogs, and large wading birds such as herons and egrets.

All turtles **LAY EGGS.**

**FACTS**

**HOME**
shallow, slow-moving water in most of North America

**FOOD**
plants, fish, insects, and crayfish

**BABIES**
4 to 15 eggs at a time

**SIZE**

**Do you prefer to finger-paint or paint with a brush? Why?**

# INDIAN NARROW-HEADED
# SOFTSHELL TURTLE

## This turtle does not have a hard shell.

**FACTS**

**HOME**
deep water in
freshwater rivers
in southern Asia

**FOOD**
mainly fish, crabs,
shrimp, frogs, and other
small animals; some-
times plants

**BABIES**
60 to 190 eggs at a time

**SIZE**

The carapace of a softshell turtle is not covered by hard plates like most turtles' shells. It is covered by leathery skin instead.

Indian narrow-headed softshell turtles spend most of their time buried in sand at the bottom of rivers. They stay hidden and wait for prey to pass nearby. This turtle has a very long neck. When a tasty fish swims by, the turtle quickly stretches out its neck to catch dinner with its mouth.

This turtle breathes by **STRETCHING** its neck so that just the tip of its **NOSE POPS UP** above the water's **SURFACE.**

Female narrow-headed **SOFTSHELL TURTLES** only come ashore to **LAY EGGS.**

**Can you think of an animal with a name that starts with the letter *g* that also has a very long neck?**

# MATAMATA

## This turtle could be mistaken for a pile of leaves.

Bumps, lumps, and spikes cover the matamata's dark yellowish brown carapace. Its head is shaped like a triangle and looks like a dead leaf. The matamata's looks help it hide from its prey.

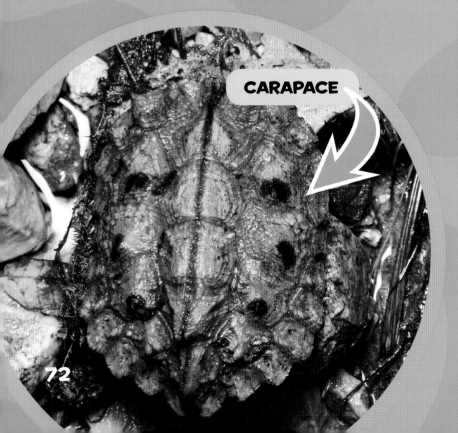

CARAPACE

A matamata sucks its prey into its mouth like a vacuum cleaner. This turtle swallows food whole. *Gulp!*

This reptile has a lot of **NICKNAMES,** including **NEEDLE-NOSE** and **LEAFHEAD.**

### FACTS

**HOME**
muddy bottoms of slow-moving streams, marshes, and swamps of northern South America and Trinidad and Tobago

**FOOD**
mostly fish; also insects, shellfish, and other small animals

**BABIES**
12 to 28 eggs at a time

**SIZE**

The **MATAMATA** belongs to a group of turtles called **SIDE-NECKED TURTLES.**

How would you describe what this turtle looks like to someone who has never seen it?

# EASTERN BOX TURTLE

### Box turtles can close up tight like a box.

Most male eastern box turtles have **RED EYES,** while most females have **YELLOW EYES.**

**What color are your eyes?**

**CLOSED UP TIGHT!**

If a raccoon, fox, or other predator starts to attack it, a box turtle pulls in its head, legs, and tail. Then it snaps shut its shell. This reptile's tough shell is very hard for any attacker to open. Most predators give up, so the turtle inside almost always survives.

Box turtles have only slightly webbed feet. They rarely swim, but they do soak in puddles. Most of their time is spent on land.

**FACTS**

**HOME**
woodlands, grasslands, and marshy areas, often near ponds or streams, in the eastern U.S.

**FOOD**
earthworms, slugs, insects, berries, flowers, and more

**BABIES**
1 to 11 eggs at a time

**SIZE**

Box turtles often **COOL OFF** in **SHADY PUDDLES.**

A box turtle can live **100 YEARS.**

75

# HERMANN'S TORTOISE

## This tortoise hibernates under a pile of leaves during the winter.

When a Hermann's tortoise crawls out of its hibernating spot in the early spring, it looks for a mate. A couple of months later, the female tortoise digs a hole and lays her eggs. She covers them by refilling the hole with dirt.

The eggs usually hatch in September, and the baby tortoises dig their way out of the nest. For the first five years, the young tortoises do not go far from their nest. It can take years for their shells to harden completely, so they need to be able to scoot into their den to escape predators.

There is a **SPIKE** on the end of its **TAIL.**

SPIKE

**FACTS**

**HOME**
forests, dry meadows, rocky hills, and farm- land in southern Europe

**FOOD**
mostly dandelions, clovers, and other plants

**BABIES**
2 to 12 eggs at a time

**SIZE**

Hermann's tortoises find a **SHADY SHELTER** when the sun gets too **HOT.**

These tortoises usually hatch in September. In what month were you born?

77

# GALÁPAGOS
# GIANT TORTOISE

These are the world's largest tortoises.

These **HUGE** tortoises **NAP** about **16 HOURS** each day.

DOME-SHAPED TORTOISE

Not all Galápagos tortoises look alike. Tortoises on some islands have shells shaped like a saddle, with a notch, or cutout, at the front. These tortoises also have long necks and legs. They are called saddlebacks. A saddleback can raise its head and stretch its legs high enough to eat plants growing up off the ground.

**FACTS**

**HOME**
grassy, dry lowlands and wetter highlands on the Galápagos Islands, off the shore of Ecuador, in South America

**FOOD**
plants such as cactus, grass, flowers, and fruits

**BABIES**
2 to 16 eggs at a time

**SIZE**

Tortoises on other islands have shorter necks and legs. They are called dome-shaped tortoises. Their shells don't have a notch, so these tortoises cannot lift their head as high as the saddleback tortoises can. They graze on plants like grasses that grow close to the ground.

SADDLEBACK TORTOISE

**GALÁPAGO** is a **SPANISH** word for **"TORTOISE."**

79

Here are a few of the more than **300 SPECIES OF TURTLES AND TORTOISES** found around the world.

BLACK-KNOBBED MAP TURTLE

RADIATED TORTOISE

LEOPARD TORTOISE

INDIAN STAR TORTOISE

PIG-NOSED TURTLE

ORNATE WOOD TURTLE

81

# CHAPTER 4
# ANCIENT SWIMMERS

The group of reptiles in this chapter is called crocodilians. Crocodilians have been around since the time of the dinosaurs.

# AMERICAN ALLIGATOR

## Mother alligators protect their babies.

### FACTS

**HOME**
freshwater rivers, lakes, and marshes in the southeastern U.S.

**FOOD**
fish, turtles, and small mammals

**BABIES**
20 to 60 eggs at a time

**SIZE**

The **ANCESTORS** of today's alligators lived at the same time that **DINOSAURS ROAMED EARTH.**

The **ALLIGATOR** is one of the **LARGEST REPTILES** in North America.

Most baby reptiles are on their own from the time they hatch. American alligators are different.

A mother alligator builds a nest made of mud and plants on dry land near a river or lake. After she lays her eggs in the nest, she covers them with plants. This keeps the eggs warm.

When the eggs hatch, the mother digs the peeping baby alligators out of the nest. Then she gently carries them in her mouth, a few at a time, to the water. They can swim right away. The babies stay near their mother for about two years.

## How many other animals can you name that make a nest for their eggs?

**HOME**
swamps in parts of
western Africa

**FOOD**
mainly fish, frogs, toads,
and crustaceans

**BABIES**
10 to 14 eggs at a time

**SIZE**

The **MAIN PREDATOR** of a full-grown dwarf crocodile is a larger species of **CROCODILE.**

# DWARF CROCODILE
## This crocodile is small but tough.

This little crocodile has more predators than bigger crocodilians. But it has extra protection. Its whole body is covered by tough scales. Unlike most other crocodiles, even its belly is covered with them.

The dwarf crocodile's webbed toes and flattened tail help it swim. Its eyes and nose are on top of its head. This allows it to see and breathe while it floats just under the surface. Floating helps hide the crocodile from predators— and from prey.

**Do you like to swim underwater? Why or why not?**

**BABY DWARF CROCODILES** stay with their **MOTHER** for a few weeks, and then they are **OFF ON THEIR OWN.**

HATCHING CROCODILE

WEBBED TOES

"SALTIE" is a **NICKNAME** for saltwater **CROCODILES.**

The saltwater crocodile has the **STRONGEST KNOWN BITE** of any living **ANIMAL.**

**What nicknames can you make up for some of the other animals in this book?**

# SALTWATER CROCODILE

## This crocodile is the world's largest living reptile.

A saltwater crocodile hunts almost anything that moves. For prey in the water, such as a shark, the crocodile sneaks up on it underwater. Once it is close—*swoosh!*—the crocodile lunges up to grab its meal.

For prey on land, such as a water buffalo getting a drink, the crocodile quietly swims close to shore. Suddenly, it bursts out of the water, grabs the buffalo, and drags it into the water. The reptile holds its prey underwater until it drowns.

**FACTS**

**HOME**
saltwater and freshwater areas in eastern India, Southeast Asia, and northern Australia and surrounding islands

**FOOD**
almost any animal, including waterbirds, sea turtles, sharks, monkeys, and deer

**BABIES**
40 to 60 eggs at a time

**SIZE**

A **SALTWATER CROCODILE** can stay underwater for more than an hour before coming to the surface.

89

# SPECTACLED CAIMAN

## Baby caimans have babysitters.

A female spectacled caiman builds a nest when she is ready to lay her eggs. She protects her eggs until they hatch, which takes about three months. The mother helps her hatchlings find their way to water close to the nest.

Other caimans usually live nearby and also have new babies. Often one mother "babysits" other caimans' babies. The moms take turns hunting for food and guarding the little caimans.

The **BONES** around a caiman's **EYES** make it look like it is **WEARING SPECTACLES,** or glasses. That is how it got its name.

Adult caimans are **DARK GREEN.** Baby caimans are **YELLOW** with **BLACK SPOTS** and bands.

## FACTS

**HOME**
freshwater and salt-water in parts of Central and South America

**FOOD**
insects, fish, lizards, snakes, birds, and other small animals

**BABIES**
20 to 40 eggs at a time

**SIZE**

Caimans stay near their mother for protection for about a year and a half. By then, they have grown big enough that most predators leave them alone. Then the young caimans go off on their own.

## Do you like it when a babysitter takes care of you?

The male gharial has a **BUMP** at the end of his nose called a **GHARA.** Males use it to **BLOW BUBBLES** to impress female gharials.

A gharial **SWIMS** better than it **WALKS.** On land, its **SHORT LEGS** cannot lift its heavy body off the ground, so it **SCOOTS ON ITS TUMMY.**

Do you like to eat fish? Why or why not?

# GHARIAL

## This crocodilian's long jaws are perfect for catching fish.

The gharial's long, narrow jaws hold more than 100 sharp teeth. Its teeth work perfectly to catch slimy, slippery fish. A gharial sometimes floats at the water's surface. It waits for a meal to swim by. *Snap!* The gharial catches the fish and swallows it headfirst.

Another way a gharial hunts is to swim underwater, slowly sweeping its head and jaws back and forth until it feels a fish. *Snap!* The gharial's jaws move with lightning speed and capture the fish. *Gulp!* The reptile swallows the fish whole.

### FACTS

**HOME**
freshwater rivers in parts of Bangladesh and Nepal and northern India

**FOOD**
mostly fish

**BABIES**
28 to 60 eggs at a time

**SIZE**

93

# CHAPTER 5

# AWESOME AMPHIBIANS

This chapter is about amphibians, including frogs and toads, salamanders, and caecilians.

# BLUE-SIDED TREE FROG

## This tree frog is more than just blue.

Female blue-sided tree frogs **LAY THEIR EGGS** on the underside of **LEAVES.** They choose leaves that hang over water. When the **EGGS HATCH,** the tadpoles **PLOP DOWN** into the **WATER** below.

EGGS

The blue-sided tree frog lives mainly in trees. All its fingers and toes have big, round discs on the ends. These discs act like suction cups. They help the tree frog cling to branches and twigs as it climbs around looking for food.

There are more than **800 SPECIES** of tree **FROGS.** Most of them are quite **SMALL.** Their size allows them to **CLIMB** on leaves and twigs.

How many different colors can you count on this frog?

97

A reticulated glass frog could **FIT ON A QUARTER.**

# RETICULATED GLASS FROG

## This frog's belly is see-through.

A female glass frog lays her eggs in a clump under a leaf. The male frog guards the eggs all day and night.

The spots on the back of an adult glass frog look a lot like the little clump of eggs. Scientists think this may trick predators, such as wasps, that are looking for frog eggs to eat.

When a wasp swoops in, the male frog guards the eggs.

**EGGS**

Male frogs **WRESTLE** each other to protect their **TERRITORY.**

**FACTS**

**HOME**
rainforests in Colombia, Ecuador, Costa Rica, and Panama

**FOOD**
insects and other small animals

**BABIES**
about 35 eggs at a time

**SIZE**

**Why do you think this frog is called a glass frog?**

MALE goliath frogs make a loud WHISTLING noise to call FEMALES.

Can you whistle like a male goliath frog?

# GOLIATH FROG

## This is the largest frog in the world.

A goliath frog is about the size of a house cat! It spends most of its time in water, but sometimes it climbs onto rocks to sit in the sun. The frog's greenish brown color helps it blend in with moss-covered rocks.

Adult goliath frogs also come ashore at night to look for food. Young frogs mostly stay underwater.

Female goliath frogs lay their eggs on plants growing underwater on a river bottom. Even though they will grow up to be huge, goliath frog tadpoles are about the same size as the tadpoles of other frogs.

**FACTS**

**HOME**
fast-flowing rivers in rainforests in Cameroon and Equatorial Guinea in Africa

**FOOD**
worms, spiders, dragonflies, locusts, small frogs, baby turtles, and other small animals

**BABIES**
several hundred eggs at a time

**SIZE**

A colorful group of more than **300 SPECIES OF FROGS CALLED POISON DART FROGS** live in the rainforests of Central and South America. Here are just a few of these brightly colored amphibians.

YELLOW-BANDED POISON DART FROG

BLUE POISON DART FROG

PHANTASMAL POISON DART FROG

GOLDEN POISON DART FROG

RED-BACKED POISON DART FROG

Common **TOADS** are usually brown, but they can also be **BLACK, GREEN,** or **YELLOW.**

# COMMON TOAD

## This toad's bumpy skin contains poison.

# FROGS VS. TOADS

Toads are a special kind of frog. There are a few differences between most frogs and toads.

## FROGS

- Most frogs live in water.
- Frogs have teeth.
- A frog's skin is smooth and slimy.

## TOADS

- Toads live on land.
- Toads do not have teeth.
- A toad's skin is bumpy and dry.

### FACTS

**HOME**
woodlands, grasslands, and near ponds in much of Europe and northern Africa

**FOOD**
ants and other insects; earthworms, slugs, spiders, snails, and other small animals

**BABIES**
thousands of eggs at a time

**SIZE**

When a fox or other predator pounces on a common toad, the toad releases its secret weapon. Its skin oozes a yucky-tasting poison!

As soon as the fox tastes the poison, it spits out the toad and trots off to find something better to eat!

# CANE TOAD

## This toad is one of the world's largest.

**FACTS**

**HOME**
open grassland and woodland in southern Texas, in the U.S.; Mexico; much of Central and South America; Australia and other places

**FOOD**
insects, frogs, other small animals; dead animals

**BABIES**
thousands at a time

**SIZE**

A cane toad's huge appetite matches its size. This toad is not a picky eater. It even eats other cane toads! The cane toad's best defense against most predators is poison. Its skin has a poison that makes many enemies get very sick or even die.

There are a few animals, such as certain fish, caimans, and snakes, that are not affected by the poison. The toad has another trick to try to escape these predators. It stands up tall by stretching its legs out straight, takes in a huge breath of air to puff up, and tries to scare away its attacker by looking bigger than it really is.

The big **CANE TOAD,** its **EGGS,** and its **TADPOLES** are **POISONOUS.**

**Can you try to look bigger, just like a cane toad does?**

# RINGED CAECILIAN

## It is not an earthworm. It is not a snake. It is an amphibian!

**SAY MY NAME:**
sih-SIL-yen

After a mother caecilian lays her eggs, she begins to grow a thick outer layer of skin filled with fat.

Her hatchlings have teeth that are shaped like spoons. They use their teeth to eat their mother's skin—this does not hurt her. The hatchlings nibble for a few minutes, all at once.

Their next meal is in about three days. By that time, their mother has grown a new layer of her special, fatty skin for them to eat. She regrows this skin until the young caecilians are a few weeks old.

CAECILIAN MOTHER AND HATCHLINGS

## FACTS

**HOME**
tropical forests, savan-
nas, grasslands, and
farmland east of the
Andes Mountains in
South America

**FOOD**
insects, worms, and
small snails

**BABIES**
5 to 16 eggs at a time

**SIZE**

The ringed
caecilian lives
**UNDERGROUND.**
It **DIGS** with
its **HEAD.**

# How would you move to show how a caecilian digs underground?

A hellbender's **BODY IS FLAT.** Its shape helps it **FIT UNDER ROCKS** to **HIDE** at the **BOTTOM** of streams.

# HELLBENDER

This salamander is the largest amphibian in North America.

Hellbenders live in the water. They stay in streams and rivers their whole lives. They choose areas with large, flat rocks and fast-moving water. The rocks provide shelter.

Fast-moving water has more oxygen mixed into it than still water does. As a river or stream flows, the splashing and bubbling of the moving water mixes air, which has oxygen, into the water.

Hellbenders breathe mostly through their skin underwater, so they need water with a lot of oxygen.

**FACTS**

**HOME**
fast-flowing, rocky streams and rivers in parts of the eastern U.S.

**FOOD**
mainly crayfish; also small fish, worms, and insects

**BABIES**
200 to 400 eggs at a time

**SIZE**

## Can you name any other animals that live in streams and rivers?

# CALIFORNIA SLENDER
# SALAMANDER
## This tiny salamander lives on land.

This kind of salamander usually **STAYS WITHIN AN AREA** about the **SIZE OF A BATHTUB.**

The California slender salamander **HATCHES ON LAND** as a **TINY VERSION** of an **ADULT.**

The California slender salamander is only about as long as your hand. It lives in forests, underneath logs, rocks, and leaves on the ground.

This little amphibian can only breathe through its skin. It stays in areas that are cool and damp. A salamander's skin has to stay moist for it to be able to breathe. The salamander's favorite time to move around is right after it rains.

## What is the farthest you have ever traveled from your home?

### FACTS

**HOME**
forests and grasslands in mountains, mainly along the coast of California, and in a small area of southern Oregon

**FOOD**
insects, spiders, snails, and other tiny animals

**BABIES**
4 to 13 eggs at a time

**SIZE**

113

# FIRE SALAMANDER

## This amphibian gives birth to live young.

A mother fire salamander's eggs stay inside her body until the larvae, or babies, are ready to hatch.

At that point, one of two things happen. Some females give birth in water to larval babies. They do not look like their mother yet. The larvae stay in the water until they grow into fully developed salamanders. Other females give birth to young that are already fully developed. They look just like mom.

**FACTS**

**HOME**
woodlands and ponds or streams in parts of Europe and the Middle East

**FOOD**
slugs, earthworms, beetles, and other small animals

**BABIES**
2 to 20 at a time

**SIZE**

**GILLS**

**LARVAL FIRE SALAMANDER**

Gills are part of a fire salamander larva's body. **GILLS TAKE OXYGEN OUT OF WATER,** allowing the larva to breathe underwater.

This salamander's bright **COLOR** and **PATTERN WARN** predators that it is **POISONOUS.**

# KAISER'S MOUNTAIN NEWT

This colorful salamander's big eyes see well in and out of water.

FEMALES **LAY** their **EGGS** on rocks **UNDERWATER** in streams.

Kaiser's mountain newts spend most of their lives on the ground in mountain forests. For a couple of months in the spring, they move into cold streams to find mates and lay eggs. Their eyesight is excellent both on land and underwater.

Scientists do not know a lot about this newt. It lives in a place that is very difficult to get to—in and around only a few streams in one mountain range.

Kaiser's mountain newt **LARVAE** take about **FOUR MONTHS** to **CHANGE** into newts that look like their **PARENTS.**

**FACTS**

**HOME**
a few cold mountain streams and woodlands in Iran

**FOOD**
worms, insects, and other small animals

**BABIES**
up to 60 eggs at a time

**SIZE**

**Which of the four salamanders you have read about so far is your favorite? Why?**

You have read about salamanders in the last several pages. **HERE ARE A FEW MORE OF THE MORE THAN 700 SALAMANDER SPECIES.**

AXOLOTL

ARBOREAL SALAMANDER

LONG-TAILED SALAMANDER

BLUE-SPOTTED SALAMANDER

TIGER SALAMANDER

# ANIMAL MAP

**Use this world map to see** on which continents the animals featured in this book can be found in the wild.

ARCTIC

NORTH AMERICA

PACIFIC OCEAN

ATLANTIC OCEAN

EQUATOR

SOUTH AMERICA

ATLANTIC OCEAN

### NORTH AMERICA
Alligator snapping turtle
American alligator
Arizona coral snake
Blue-sided tree frog
Boa constrictor
California slender salamander
Cane toad
Common garter snake
Eastern box turtle
Eastern diamondback rattlesnake
Green anole
Green iguana
Hellbender
Painted turtle
Reticulated glass frog
Spectacled caiman

### ATLANTIC OCEAN
Hawksbill sea turtle

### PACIFIC OCEAN
Banded sea krait
Hawksbill sea turtle

### SOUTH AMERICA
Boa constrictor
Cane toad
Galápagos giant tortoise
Green iguana
Marine iguana
Matamata
Reticulated glass frog
Ringed caecilian
Spectacled caiman

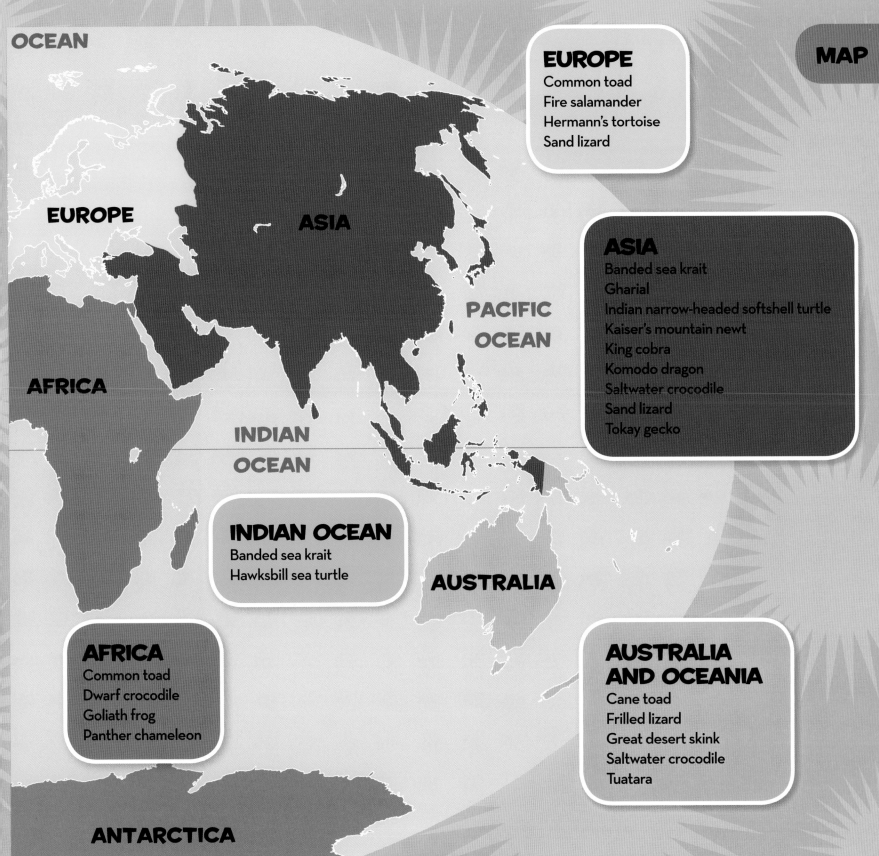

OCEAN

EUROPE

ASIA

PACIFIC
OCEAN

AFRICA

INDIAN
OCEAN

AUSTRALIA

ANTARCTICA

**EUROPE**
Common toad
Fire salamander
Hermann's tortoise
Sand lizard

**ASIA**
Banded sea krait
Gharial
Indian narrow-headed softshell turtle
Kaiser's mountain newt
King cobra
Komodo dragon
Saltwater crocodile
Sand lizard
Tokay gecko

**INDIAN OCEAN**
Banded sea krait
Hawksbill sea turtle

**AFRICA**
Common toad
Dwarf crocodile
Goliath frog
Panther chameleon

**AUSTRALIA
AND OCEANIA**
Cane toad
Frilled lizard
Great desert skink
Saltwater crocodile
Tuatara

# PARENT TIPS

Extend your child's experience beyond the pages of this book. Visits to a zoo, aquarium, wetland, park, or nature center are several great ways to continue satisfying your child's curiosity about reptiles and amphibians. Here are some other activities you can do with National Geographic's *Little Kids First Big Book of Reptiles and Amphibians*.

## GO ON A HERP WALK
### (OBSERVATION)

Herpetology is the study of reptiles and amphibians. Plan an outing to look for these animals. Head to a wetland park or neighborhood pond, for example, to find frogs, turtles, and snakes. Encourage your child to think about where some likely spots are to look for reptiles and amphibians. Spring is a great time to spot frogs and toads: follow their calls. On a sunny day, check logs in wetlands for turtles warming themselves. If there is a nature center where you are exploring, ask for a checklist of the reptiles and amphibians associated with the area.

## SILLY JOKES
### (HUMOR)

Telling jokes, riddles, and tongue twisters are great ways to get you and your child giggling. Look for reptile- and amphibian-related jokes online or in joke books, or make up your own. Suggest that your child make up her own, too. Here are a few to get started:

Q: What is a frog's favorite music?
A: Hip-hop!

AMERICAN ALLIGATOR

Q: What do you call a snake that builds things?
A: A boa constructor!

Q: When does a lizard say "moo"?
A: When it is learning a new language!

## CONCENTRATION
(MEMORY)

Play a game of concentration with a deck of cards you and your child make. On index cards, draw the simple shapes of 10 of the animals in this book. Make duplicates, so you have two of each shape. Have your child decorate all the animals in pairs that look alike. Then place the 20 shuffled cards facedown. Take turns turning over two each. If they match, keep them. If they don't match, turn them back over. When all the cards are matched, count to see who has the most pairs.

## MAKE A PAPER SNAKE
(ARTS AND CRAFTS)

Using colored construction paper, help your child make his own snake. Cut the paper into equal strips, about eight per sheet of paper. Have your child staple or glue the ends of a strip to create a loop. Thread the next strip through the first loop, and connect the ends. Continue until your "snake" is as long as your child wants it to be. Cut out two triangular shapes (with rounded corners). One should be larger than the other. Have your child draw a face on the larger triangle. He might like to glue googly eyes on the snake's face. A short strip of red paper makes a great snake tongue. Glue the face onto one end of the snake. Use the other triangle for the snake's tail. Your child might also enjoy adding some finishing touches by decorating his snake's whole body using crayons, markers, glitter, and sequins.

# GLOSSARY

**ALGAE:** a group of organisms that usually grow in water, such as kelp and other seaweed

**CRUSTACEANS:** a large group of animals, such as lobsters and crabs, with a hard outer skeleton, pairs of legs or claws on each segment of the body, and two pairs of antennae

**ECTOTHERM:** an animal with a body that cannot make its own heat, and that depends on its surrounding environment for warmth

**ENDOTHERM:** an animal with a body that can produce its own heat

**MAMMALS:** a group of vertebrate animals, including humans, that are endothermic, breathe air, have hair, and nurse their young

**POISON:** a toxin that causes harm when the victim swallows it, absorbs it through skin, or breathes it in

GREEN TREE FROG CATCHING A HAWK MOTH

**POISONOUS:** an animal or plant that delivers a toxin when touched or eaten by the victim

**PREDATOR:** an animal that hunts other animals (prey) for food

**PREY:** an animal that a predator hunts and kills for food

**SPECIES:** a category, or unique kind, of animal or plant

**TOXIN:** a poison or venom

KOMODO DRAGON

**HAWKSBILL SEA TURTLE**

**VENOM:** a toxin that causes harm when injected through a bite or a sting

**VENOMOUS:** an animal or plant that delivers a toxin by injecting it into the victim

**VERTEBRATE:** animal that has a spinal column, or backbone

# ADDITIONAL RESOURCES

### BOOKS

Hoena, Blake. *Everything Reptiles.* National Geographic Kids Books, 2016.

Howell, Catherine Herbert. *Ultimate Explorer Field Guide: Reptiles and Amphibians.* National Geographic Kids Books, 2016.

Wilsdon, Christina. *Ultimate Reptileopedia.* National Geographic Kids Books, 2015.

### WEBSITES

A note for parents and teachers: For more information on this topic, you can visit these websites with your young readers.

amphibiaweb.org

animaldiversity.org

nationalgeographic.com/animals/reptiles

nationalzoo.si.edu/animals/exhibits /reptile-discovery-center

# INDEX